Original title:
Forest Floor Musings

Copyright © 2025 Creative Arts Management OÜ
All rights reserved.

Author: Rosalie Bradford
ISBN HARDBACK: 978-1-80566-637-0
ISBN PAPERBACK: 978-1-80566-922-7

The Hidden Haven

Beneath the leaves, a squirrel hides,
With acorns stored in secret tides.
He thinks he's clever, oh what a feat,
While birds above just call him 'Sweet'.

The mushrooms giggle, a funny bunch,
With caps like hats, they love their lunch.
They share their stories, so sly and quick,
While ants parade, all marching thick.

Silent Stories in the Dirt

In the soil, whispers start to throng,
A worm confesses he's quite strong.
He wriggles and wiggles, a claim so bold,
While beetles chuckle as tales unfold.

A twig once tripped a clumsy hare,
Who stumbled then rolled, without a care.
The laughter echoed, it rang so clear,
In the dirt, joy blooms without a fear.

Twists of Twine

A vine got tangled, oh what a sight,
Wraps around branches with all its might.
The trees are chuckling, they sway and shake,
As the vine mutters, 'For goodness' sake!'

A rabbit hops by, with snacks in tow,
He stumbles and slips, a comedy show.
The twine just giggles, with a twisty grin,
Nature's own prankster, let the fun begin!

Mushrooms and Musings

Mushrooms gather for a tea so grand,
With cups of dew from a gentle hand.
They swap wild tales of creatures bold,
While insects listen, their stories told.

A snail slides slow, with thoughts to share,
About his travels, oh how rare!
The fungi laugh as the grass nods along,
In their secret nook, where all belong.

Crawl Spaces of Creation

In shadows deep where critters hide,
A worm with dreams takes a cosmic ride.
He shifts the dirt, he bends the light,
And giggles softly at a passing sprite.

A spider spins tales of fluff and dread,
While ants throw parties with crumbs they've bred.
"Dance on my web, you silly flies!"
"Just watch your step, or the world goodbye!"

Iridescent Insects' Whispers

Beetles convene for a midnight chat,
"Did you see the snail? He's got no hat!"
"Can you believe he's still in his shell?
It's a mere fashion faux pas, do tell!"

A grasshopper jumps like a pro at a show,
While crickets compose a tune, nice and slow.
"Don't you fret, it's a party tonight,
We'll dance 'til dawn, till we take flight!"

The Quiet Rebirth of Earth

Skunks wear colognes of graceful delight,
While mushrooms throw shade in the soft moonlight.
Pine needles whisper, then giggle, then sway,
As the owls comment on the listing of prey.

The sun peeks in, through branches it creeps,
Awakening beings from their cozy sleeps.
"Did you hear that joke?" said a nearby fox,
"Why do trees listen? They hate talking rocks!"

Sounds of Serpentine Shadows

A snake on a quest with no shoes to wear,
Slithers through grass with a flick and a flare.
"Hey! Look at me!" he hisses with glee,
"King of the underbrush, can't you see?"

The shadows applaud as he wiggles along,
While frogs in the pond sing a colorful song.
"Catch me if you can, my slippery friend!"
"And don't forget to bring snacks at the end!"

Patterns of Petals

In blooms so bright, the bees all tease,
They dance and twirl with such great ease.
Each petal's path, a story spun,
Oh, nature's whim, it's all just fun!

But then comes rain, a twist of fate,
With muddy shoes, I can't be late!
A flower slips, it gives a shout,
"Watch your step! Now look who's out!"

The Stories of the Soil

The worms debate in underground chats,
Complaining of the curious cats.
With a squirm and a giggle, they share the news,
"Don't dig too deep or lose your shoes!"

Old roots gossip about the trees,
"Did you see that squirrel, what a tease!"
Life below, so full of grins,
Who knew dirt could hold such wins?

Roots of Reverie

Beneath the trunks in whispers low,
The roots exchange their tales, you know.
One claims to touch the sky so wide,
While another boasts of the lost bugs inside!

With giggling mushrooms chiming in,
"Hey, was that a mushroom or a hat for a chin?"
In this wild world, we find our quirky pals,
Reverie blooms where laughter never stalls.

Solitude of the Undergrowth

In the thicket meek and shy,
Where groundhogs sip tea and rabbits sigh,
A hedgehog dressed in Sunday wear,
Whispers secrets without a care.

Beneath the ferns, a party brews,
With dancing dandelions, they share their views.
"Let's spin and sway till morning light!"
"Oops! Watch out for that toad! What a fright!"

Secrets in the Underbrush

Beneath the leaves, a squirrel's joke,
A mushroom giggles, but won't choke.
The ants parade with tiny hats,
While grasshoppers dance, and no one chats.

Toadstools whisper secrets, oh so grand,
A snail's slow race—who planned this band?
The critters chuckle, play all day,
In the underbrush, they laugh and sway.

The Soft Lullaby of Moss

Mossy blankets, oh so thick,
They cradle whispers, soft and quick.
A sleepy worm hums a tune,
While crickets cruise beneath the moon.

Frogs croak low in jolly glee,
As butterflies sip from cups of tea.
Nature's choir sings a sweet rhyme,
As laughing leaves play hide and climb.

Nature's Gentle Tapestry

Threads of ivy weave a tale,
As chipmunks plot their tiny trail.
Berries wink with a luscious grin,
While dandelions wear crowns of sin.

Spider webs glisten, catching dew,
The bees are gossiping, who knew?
A butterfly winks, then flits away,
In nature's quilt, the mischief will stay.

Dappled Light on Humble Soil

Sunlight dances through the green,
Beneath the ferns, mischief is seen.
Worms hold meetings, share their woes,
As playful shadows steal the shows.

A beetle boasts of its fine shell,
While sleepy flowers begin to swell.
The roots below giggle in delight,
As dappled light fades into night.

The Litter's Lullaby

A candy wrapper sings in glee,
The squirrels dance a jig, quite free.
Old soda cans hum a tune,
As frogs croak out beneath the moon.

A tumbleweed plays peek-a-boo,
With dandelions, all askew.
Plastic bags twirl in a chase,
What a wild, wacky place!

Leaves whistle as they sway and spin,
While pebbles join the playful din.
Nature's jesters on display,
Litter's lullaby leads the way.

So, if you hear a rustle near,
Just know it's fun and not a fear.
It's the joyful mess that brings a smile,
Nature's laughter, mile by mile.

Echoes of the Evergreen

Pine cones drop with comedic flair,
Knocking squirrels right off their chair.
Trees whisper jokes in the breezy air,
While mushrooms giggle without a care.

Acorns roll and play a game,
Telling tales, none quite the same.
Chipmunks chuckle at silly sights,
In a realm where laughter ignites.

Branches nod with a knowing grin,
As wind rushes, it's all in the spin.
The trunks stand tall with wisdom vast,
While prancing critters run fast.

Listen close, you'll hear the mirth,
In echoes of laughter, it's pure earth.
Amongst the tall, where shadows blend,
A comedy show that has no end.

Shadows Beneath the Leaves

A snail made of foam takes a slide,
While beetles argue who's the best ride.
Shadows loom low, soft and sly,
As ants march by with a pie in the sky.

Grasshoppers chirp with jokes galore,
While ladybugs plead for just one more.
A cactus whispers funny truths,
About garden gnomes stealing their youths.

Underneath canopies, secrets hide,
As wise old trees chuckle with pride.
They know the punchlines, oh so sweet,
Jokes that bounce with nature's beat.

So if you stroll through the shady path,
Listen closely, embrace the laugh.
For nature's humor, wild and grand,
Is always hiding, close at hand.

Tapestry of Twigs

A tapestry of twigs interlace,
Crafting homes for critters' embrace.
Each twig a tale of past delight,
Of cheeky raccoons and their nightly flight.

Beetles wear helmets made of bark,
While ants march with their snack-filled cart.
A woven story, vivid and bright,
Of all the mischief that takes flight.

Branches giggle, weaving patterns wide,
As stems twist and twirl, side by side.
A clever design of life's great play,
In the jigsaw of nature, come what may.

So ponder the art, so random yet real,
As twigs unite with a humorous feel.
In the woods where chaos meets glee,
Behold the tapestry, wild and free.

The Symphony of Soil

In the dirt, a worm did squirm,
He danced and twirled, oh what a term.
A beetle played a tiny drum,
While ants hummed loud, 'We're never glum!'

A snail slid by, all slimy and slow,
He said, "I'm a racer, just took it low!"
The mushrooms giggled in shades of brown,
While daisies muttered, "Where's our crown?"

A hazel nut began to roll,
Declared, "I'm off to find my soul!"
But tripped on roots and fell with a thud,
Then laughed aloud, "Well, that was mud!"

In this patch, all creatures convene,
Music of laughter, none so mean.
What a racket, what a fun place,
On the ground, we strike a happy space.

Beneath the Bark

Beneath the bark, the critters play,
Squirrels chase in a funny way.
A raccoon slipped on a fallen leaf,
And chuckled loud at his own grief.

A tree frog croaked a silly tune,
While dancing shadows made them swoon.
The woodpecker drummed on a hollow stump,
All joined in, creating a thump.

Mice gathered 'round for a grand tale,
Of cheese so big it tilted the scale.
But the cheese was fake, just a buttercup,
They shrugged it off and filled their cup.

In this hideout, the laughter flows,
Amongst the roots and downy snows.
Wild tales linger, and time holds fast,
Under the bark, life's a fun blast.

Ferns and Fables

A fern sat tall with a whimsical grin,
Told fables of time when frogs would spin.
She waved her fronds, made shadows dance,
While slips of grass joined in the chance.

An old toad spoke of a regal worm,
Who wore a cloak shaped like a fern.
He claimed he ruled the garden's heart,
But tripped on roots, not too smart!

The bees buzzed in with a gossip thread,
They spilled the tales that semi-floated overhead.
'You won't believe who tickled a twig,'
The flowers laughed, 'Oh, that is big!'

With ferns as crowns and smiles so wide,
In this realm, there's nowhere to hide.
Behind each leaf, a chuckle blooms,
In this patch, joy is deeper than tombs.

Nightfall's Gentle Carpet

As nightfall creeps, the critters jive,
In cozy nooks, they dance and thrive.
A mouse in socks starts a wiggly show,
While fireflies glow like stars below.

A hedgehog strummed on a twiggy lute,
With rhymes about a dancing boot.
The crickets chirped in playful tune,
Recalling sunlit afternoons.

Amongst the shadows, giggles spark,
As creatures play and ignite the dark.
A raccoon in ribbons twirls with glee,
Confetti of leaves floats down like a spree.

So let the night be a welcome sheet,
Where tales are told and friends do meet.
In this gentle carpet, laughter's found,
With every rustle, joy's unbound.

Nature's Quiet Confessions

Amidst the leaves, a squirrel squeaks,
His acorn jokes hide in soft creaks.
The grass blades giggle as I walk by,
They've seen more falls than I can try.

A snail races with a surprising pace,
Winning at slow, it's his favorite race.
The mushrooms chuckle, popping their heads,
"Who brought the snacks? It's time to be fed!"

Secrets of the Sedge

The sedge whispers secrets, soft and low,
Did you hear the tale of the dancing crow?
He twirled on his toes with such flair and might,
His friends just clucked, it was quite a sight.

A butterfly laughed while sipping some dew,
"Life's too short, just try something new!"
While ants held a meeting, plotting their schemes,
"Let's find the crumbs, let's follow our dreams!"

Beneath the Branches

Under the branches, a hedgehog snores,
Dreaming of treats and exciting tours.
A rabbit nearby jumps in surprise,
When a twig tickles his twitching eyes.

The wind whispers jokes, a playful tease,
"Why don't trees ever speak? They have no knees!"
In this lively place, laughter abounds,
With every rustle and chirp, joy resounds.

The Poetry of Decay

Leaves fall gracefully, doing a dance,
Whispering softly, they take a chance.
Mushrooms sprout where the shadows play,
"Guess we're the art in decay today!"

A beetle rolls a tiny ball near,
"Who knew my job would be full of cheer?"
Nature's a jester in hues of brown,
With giggles and grins, she wears her crown.

Life Among the Ofelia

In the shade where shadows play,
I found a snail who'd lost his way.
He said, "With luck, I'll glide and twirl,"
As he practiced his slow dance whirl.

While beetles race in a manic flight,
Mice gossip 'bout mushrooms every night.
A squirrel gave a nutty quip,
As acorns did a boogie flip.

A patch of grass where daisies grin,
Holds secrets of life beneath the skin.
A toad croaked jokes about the rain,
While worms rolled in the soft terrain.

Together we laugh, the woodland crew,
In our merry realm that's fresh and new.
No one's in a race, we're here for fun,
Join us for laughter, we're never done!

Beneath the Mulch

Underneath where the soggy lies,
The critters host their grand surprise.
A party of ants in tuxedos neat,
They shuffle about on tiny feet.

A centipede flaunted his fancy shoes,
While mushrooms jived to the earthy blues.
They twirled 'round roots with such past grace,
Till slugs showed up, a slippery pace.

"Who ordered this wet and mushy scene?"
Cried a curious worm, so rarely seen.
But all was well, they danced till dawn,
An underground rave—come now, come on!

Beneath the mulch, jokes bloom and grow,
In this hidden world, there's quite a show.
Join the parade where the laughter sways,
Unraveling laughter in muddy ways!

Ruminations of the Root

Rooted deep in thoughts so light,
A tree mused on the birds in flight.
"Why do they flit while I remain?"
In reply, the wind laughed, "There's no constraint!"

"While you stand tall in charm and grace,
We zip and zoom all over the place.
You're sturdy, old chap, like a wise old sage,
We're but mere actors on this grand stage!"

A mushroom piped up, "You're lucky, dear,
We're squished and stomped, we live in fear!"
But the roots just wiggled, cracked a grin,
"We've learned to laugh and let joy in!"

So let's toast to all, both low and high,
In this crazy dance beneath the sky.
With humor and glee, roots thrive and sprawl,
In this leafy realm, we're having a ball!

When the Breezes Whisper

When the breezes whisper low and sweet,
I heard a cricket tap its feet.
"Life's a stage," it gave a creak,
"Where grasshoppers juggle and fungi speak!"

A finch chirped loudly, "I'm the star!
With feathers that shine from near and far."
And a worm grinned wide, "I dig the tune,
I'm the underground maestro, let's play till noon!"

A squirrel joined in with acorns galore,
Threads of laughter began to pour.
Each little creature seized the stage,
Raising the spirits of every age.

So come join the fun when breezes sing,
With chuckles that make our hearts take wing.
In this enchanted grove, let joy unfurl,
As the woodland orchestra spins and twirls!

Murmurs of the Mycelium

Fungi whisper secrets, oh so sly,
Under the soil where the critters lie.
Mushrooms dance like they own the space,
While ants just roll their eyes in grace.

Rabbits hop and say, "What's that?"
A mushroom's joke? Or just a chat?
They giggle at the leaves up high,
While toadstools wink, and squirrels just sigh.

Grubs are gossiping, tumbling round,
Over the latest gossip they've found.
"Did you hear? The oak's got a splinter!"
Laughter erupts, the fun never's winter.

In this kingdom of dirt, all's a play,
With giggles and chuckles that lead the day.
The mycelium's laugh, a bubbling stream,
Life's playful humor is quite a dream.

The Crust of the World

Tiny beetles roll like champs on their backs,
With leaves as surfboards, they ride big cracks.
A snail slips by, says, "What a ride!"
But a worm just grins, snug inside, wide.

From the top, a squirrel throws down acorns,
Wishing to land a prize for the morns.
"They're hats now!" claims one brave little bug,
While enjoying the feast from his cozy rug.

Mice host tea parties, oh what a scene!
Inviting ants, who bring snacks evergreen.
"Is this oat-based?" one cheeky mouse scoffs,
"Next time, bring crumbs, not your leaf-stuffed fluffs!"

Under the crust, mischief stirs along,
Each creature hums their own silly song.
Laughter erupts as the sun begins to thaw,
In the land where the quirky hold the law.

The Subtle Elegance

A ladybug struts across a twig,
Dressed so fine, thinking she's big.
"Check out my spots, aren't they divine?"
While caterpillars munch in straight lines.

A dance party starts right on the grass,
With ants in tuxedos, oh what a class!
Fireflies light up their fancy affair,
The moon watches on, a silky-haired bear.

"Who's that?" asks a fly, "With the shiny shoes?"
"That's Mr. Centipede! You must be confused."
Gossip spreads quick on this buzzing street,
As grasshoppers jump to the rhythm and beat.

In this elegance, humor takes flight,
Nature's finest, bringing pure delight.
Each creature plays, in harmony bright,
Under the stars, life feels just right.

Layers of Life

Underneath the leaves, secrets are stacked,
Each layer a story, a joke intact.
Worms spin tales from the soil so deep,
While fungi chuckle, in shadows they creep.

A lizard lounges, on a sunlit rock,
Says, "Life's a hoot if you just don't clock!"
Butterflies flutter, with humor so light,
"Did you hear the one about the worm's delight?"

A cricket on harp, strums a tune so loud,
While a ladybug swishes, bright and proud.
"Oh please, not another!" the ants do plea,
As one sneaks past, yelling "I'm free!"

Layers of laughter, in shadows they throw,
In this ecosystem, a continuous show.
Life dances along, through humor's sweet strife,
Each creature a player in this quirky life.

Spiders' Secret Dwellings

In the corner, eight legs scurry,
Creating homes in such a hurry.
With webs that catch both flies and folks,
They giggle softly at our pokes.

In shadows deep, their laughter soars,
While we just stomp near secret doors.
They play a game of hide and seek,
While we jump back, with quite a squeak!

Their mansions hold the tiniest dust,
Yet, to be scared? Well, we mustn't. Trust!
So tiptoe softly, laugh out loud,
Join their webby, bouncy crowd!

But when they crawl up on your chair,
It's best to shout and act like you care.
For if they giggle and you don't flee,
You might just join their webs carefree!

Among the Fallen Foliage

Leaves crunch softly underfoot, they say,
As squirrels dance in the cabaret.
Unfortunately, I trip on a stick,
And down I go, a real slapstick!

With acorns raining like mini bombs,
I dodge their plot with goofy qualms.
The forest floor is quite the stage,
Where every tumble deserves a page!

Underfoot, the critters plot and scheme,
Twirling my legs—oh what a dream!
A world of giggles in leafy shrouds,
Where nature's humor laughs out loud.

But do beware, oh watch your step,
For a snail has dreams of becoming adept.
Just when I think, I've found my groove,
A trodden path is my best move!

Nature's Soft Palette

Colors bursting, a vivid show,
Mushrooms bobbing, a wobbly row.
In this canvas, the owls hoot,
And paintbrushes toss a noodle chute!

A yellow leaf whispers, 'Go have fun!',
While blueberries giggle, 'We're not yet done!'
With hues so bright, it's quite the flair,
Watch out for bees with wild hair!

The sunlight dances with a grin,
As shadows hide their wacky kin.
A squirrel dons a purple tie,
As butterflies giggle, oh my, oh my!

Nature's trick is in plain sight,
With every color, it's pure delight.
So splash in puddles and twirl around,
For every face here is homeward bound!

The Embrace of Earth

The earth waves softly, 'Come, take a dip!'
Where worms hold parties, let's join the trip!
With soil so rich, they roll and twirl,
Inviting us in for a muddy whirl.

With roots that tickle, they play hide and seek,
Unseen by us, they giggle and squeak.
As we stumble and tumble, they chuckle away,
Could nature be funnier? No way, no way!

In sticky embrace, we laugh and hiss,
While everyone dreams of a squishy bliss.
So wiggle your toes in this bouncy bed,
The earth's laughter lingers, till dreams are fed!

As dusk cuddles close, we sigh with glee,
Thanking the dirt for this jubilee.
All fun aside, with hearts so bright,
We leave with chuckles into the night!

Layers of Time in Twists and Folds

Underneath the rustling leaves,
Worms share gossip, never grieves.
Old acorns joke about the years,
While whispered secrets tickle ears.

Mossy hats on toadstools sway,
As beetles dance in bright array.
Fallen branches tell their tales,
Of rainy days and sunbeam trails.

Squirrels drop snacks, a buffet spread,
While rabbits argue 'bout their bed.
Nature's laughter fills the air,
A merry choir everywhere.

Pine cones giggle in delight,
As shadows play hide and seek each night.
Roots entwined in a wiggly knot,
All the woodland's laughter is hot.

Cradle of Life in Shadows Deep

Under rocks where ants parade,
Lizards flaunt their sunning grade.
Beetle fashion shows take flight,
In the shadows, a wild sight.

Mushrooms sport their polka dots,
While spiders weave their tangled knots.
A grassy stage for nimble feet,
Where critters gather for a seat.

Worms in congress pass a note,
Debating who has the best coat.
While hedgehogs hide their prickly pride,
In this bustling, funny ride.

A cricket's tune, a comic score,
Draws in the crowd for an encore.
In shadows deep, the stories weave,
Of partying life that springs from leave.

The Mandala of Nature's Debris

Twigs and leaves in swirling whirl,
In nature's art, the colors twirl.
A crumpled paper from last night's feast,
Whispers tales of a forgotten beast.

Peanut shells tell of squirrel dreams,
While green apples laugh, bursting seams.
The dance of detritus, such a sight,
In the circle of life, pure delight.

Fungi doodles on barked walls,
Echo of laughter in nature's halls.
A rabbit's waltz with stray pine cones,
Beneath the boughs, no one moans.

Chattering leaves in twilight's glow,
Invite the stars to join the show.
In this crafted mess of fun and cheer,
A tapestry of life appears.

Secrets from the Depths of Green

A chipmunk's secret, snug and tight,
 Hiding goodies from last night.
Rich debates 'bout best nuts to snack,
 In the underbrush, a lively pack.

Leaves fall down like confetti spread,
As frogs make jokes from their warm bed.
With each hop, they bump with glee,
Singing lowly, 'Come laugh with me!'

Underneath the roots, all snug,
Tadpoles whisper, feeling snug.
What dreams may sprout in this green land?
Tiny adventures, oh so grand!

In this web of life, giggles bloom,
While flowers shake off winter's gloom.
Their fragrant scents, a silly tease,
Tickling noses with nature's ease.

Timeless Tales of the Tangle

In the underbrush so dense,
A squirrel lost his little sense,
He mistook a shoe for a nut,
And now he's stuck, what's up with that?

A toad hopped in for a chat,
Asked why the shoe was wearing a hat,
"It's not a trend, but do stay near,"
Both chuckled loud, sharing a cheer.

Mossy critters rolled on by,
Wondering why the shoe could fly,
But toads don't hop from hole to hole,
When squirrels surely steal the whole.

Among the roots, they find their glee,
In tangled tales, they dance with free,
Life's a jest beneath the trees,
Where laughter sprouts like dandelions' tease.

Flickering Fancies

A firefly glowed with a twist,
Dreamt of being a glowing mist,
But when he blinked, oh dear, oh dear,
He flickered out, then reappeared.

A beetle rolled a perfect ball,
Claimed it was a tiny wall,
"It bumps and rolls, it has a charm,"
But crashed it all, and set alarm.

Acorns dropped like little bombs,
Each splash a joke, a laugh that calms,
With whispers of the night so bright,
They giggle low till morning light.

In this dim-lit whimsical place,
Where bugs and critters find their grace,
Each flickering tale a new delight,
From silly woes to laughter's flight.

The Foundation of Life

The worms below had quite a plan,
Pooling dirt for the next big band,
With beats of roots and rhymes of rain,
They made a tune, a wormy gain.

A tiny ant, with dreams so grand,
Thought he'd venture out quite unplanned,
But tripped on leaves, fell with a sigh,
"Guess I'll stick close, it's safer to lie!"

A dandelion puffed up in pride,
Said, "Here's my fluff! Come take a ride!"
But winds came waltzing, danced in delight,
Leaving behind only seeds in flight.

In this burrow where laughter sows,
Life takes root, as everyone knows,
Foundation's built on silly dreams,
Life grins wide as it brightly beams.

Blossoms of the Beneath

Underneath where shadows play,
Blooming jokes in a leafy sway,
A mushroom wearing a sunhat tall,
Said, "I'm a champ, I've got it all!"

A quirky root made quite a scene,
Claiming he's a hidden bean,
"Just plant me deep, I'll grow quite mad!",
But all he got was a gopher's lad.

Raccoons held a dinner bash,
With acorns, berries, and a dash,
They feasted well, and all agreed,
Nature's humor is the best indeed!

Amongst the giggles, bright colors thrive,
In the cradle where the wild things jive,
The blossoms sprout with a cheeky air,
A world's delight, a hearty affair.

The Scent of Earth After Rain

Puddles form a wobbly dance,
Snails move in a slow romance.
Mushrooms pop, like hats on heads,
Tiny umbrellas where worms are bred.

Worms wiggle, thinking they are slick,
Playing hide and seek, oh what a trick!
The air is fresh, like a bath for trees,
As frogs croak rhymes with utmost ease.

Leaves dripping tales of nature's cheer,
Each drop a giggle, crystal clear.
Ants parade in tidy lines,
Marching to their muddy designs.

Squirrels chatter with nuts to share,
Life is funny, if you dare stare.
A joyful mess of scents and sounds,
In this wet wonder, laughter abounds.

Meditations Among the Ferns

Ferns wave gently, like they know a joke,
Whispering secrets to a sleepy oak.
A squirrel stifles a chuckle or two,
As I trip on roots like it's all brand new.

Bumblebees buzz with a bit of flair,
While butterflies float without a care.
A ladybug winks as she strolls on by,
While ants debate if the sky is shy.

Mushrooms giggle, sprouting by the shade,
Offering spots for a cozy trade.
The breeze giggles and pulls at my hat,
Oh, nature's humor; just imagine that!

I sit and ponder, heart full of glee,
Among the ferns, the world feels free.
Nature's laugh track plays without end,
In this green sanctuary, we all blend.

Hidden Lives in the Leaf Litter

Creepy crawlies hold a grand parade,
In cozy homes that leaves have made.
A centipede grins, what's he thinking?
As twigs above seem ever blinking.

Worms play peek-a-boo, soft and round,
While pill bugs huddle, safe on the ground.
Beneath the chaos, a dance begins,
As crickets chirp, playing violins.

An ant slips past, with a crumb in tow,
While beetles bask in the sun's warm glow.
Each rustle whispers a giggly line,
In the hidden world, everything's fine.

Nature's confessions in the leaf-strewn sea,
Where every hidden life beams with glee.
In this abundant, messy affair,
I find my laughter, suspended in air.

Memories of Twisting Vines

Twisting, turning, vines embrace,
Creating a maze, oh, what a place!
Their leafy laughter tickles the breeze,
As critters navigate with utmost ease.

A chameleon poses, what a sly face,
Blending in and stealing the space.
While squirrels chase with nuts for fun,
Each dash and leap, a quirky run.

The vines weave stories like knots in string,
Of sunlit days and the joy they bring.
A bumblebee buzzes, announcing it's late,
While I giggle at nature's grand state.

Here in the twists, life feels alive,
Where laughter and wonder so easily thrive.
In the tangle of greens, spirits abound,
Memories of joy cover the ground.

Whimsy in the Wild Undergrowth

A squirrel wearing a tiny hat,
Danced round the trunk, quite chitchat.
The mushrooms giggled, all in a row,
While ants played tag in a line, you know!

A snail with a shell of sparkly gold,
Said, "Hurry up, friends, don't be too bold!"
But who could rush in a game so grand?
When the grass is soft, and the sun is planned!

Signs of Change on Softened Ground

The leaves spoke secrets, all in a whirl,
To bumblebees buzzing, giving a twirl.
"Look out for puddles!" a wise frog did croak,
While a clay pigeon squeaked, "I'm just a joke!"

The toadstools wore smiles, both wide and round,
In their caps, a tiny feast could be found.
"Fee-fi-fo-fum," sang the fairies at play,
As dew drops giggled, "It's a splish-splash day!"

A Canvas of Unspoken Stories

Under the brush of shadows so deep,
The critters gathered, not one dare sleep.
A hedgehog sighed, "I'm a real-life bard,"
While a fox piped up, "Now, isn't that hard?"

The ivy whispered tales of old,
Of sung moonlight and marigold.
"Come gather round!" the trees waved their arms,
With whispers of magic and quirky charms!

The Rhythm of Roots and Stones

In the cradle of roots, a party did start,
With rhythm of stones, it beat like a heart.
The raccoons wore hats, quite mismatched and fun,
Dancing and prancing till the day was done.

A waltz with the wind, oh, wasn't it grand?
With ladybugs twirling, hand in hand!
The oak tree thudded a heavy drum,
While the fireflies flashed, "Come on, let's hum!

Love Letters from the Land

Oh, the grass whispered secrets to me,
While a squirrel threw acorns with glee.
A snail showed up, quite late to the show,
Said, 'Better slow down before you go!'

The daisies laughed at the dandelions,
'You think you're so great, but we're the designs!'
The thorns chimed in, 'We've got quite the bite,'
While a crow cawed, 'You're wrong, I'm polite!'

Mushrooms giggled in hats so bright,
While worms wiggled, embracing the night.
Leaves fell down, joining in the fun,
Their twirling dance, oh, how they run!

Nature's jesters, a merry parade,
In the realm where laughter is made.
With twigs as our quills and mud as our ink,
We scribble our tales, making the world think!

The Hum of Hidden Harmony

Under the canopy, where shadows play,
A chatty cricket sang all day.
He boasted of tunes that could win a prize,
While a sleepy turtle rolled his eyes.

Bees buzzed gossip from flower to flower,
Claiming to have the best nectar power.
A badger chimed in with a wise old grunt,
'Bumblebees, sweet, but a bit on the blunt!'

The wind twirled around, making quite a fuss,
Shrugged her leaf jacket, said, 'It's just us!'
As the brook chuckled, splashing with flair,
'Life's a big giggle when you stop and stare!'

In this quirky world, joy intertwines,
As critters concoct their own punchlines.
With humor and mirth in each creature's heart,
We all join together, a laugh-filled art!

The Canvas of Nature

In the morning light, a painter came,
With daffodils bright, he won the game.
He flicked his brush at a passing bee,
Saying, 'Buzz off! Let me paint in peace!'

Rocks posed proudly, all covered in moss,
While ants held a meeting, flipping a toss.
They debated the best way to move a crumb,
'How many of us?' they grumbled and hummed.

A fern giggled, 'I'm the true green star!'
While a raccoon argued, 'But I'm the bizarre!'
With colors and laughter, nature unfolds,
Each stroke of joy, a story retold.

When twilight drapes her canvas serene,
The critters gather to see what's been seen.
With a chuckle and cheer, they dance in delight,
As stars poke their heads to join in the night!

Echoes of Old Roots

Deep in the soil, where the whispers stay,
The old roots chuckled, 'We're here to play!'
They shared tales of the sky and the rain,
While a toad croaked, 'You're all so vain!'

A beetle rolled by, with a hop and a spin,
Said, 'I've got secrets caught right in my skin.'
But the mushrooms jumped in, all plump and round,
'You think you're fancy? We're nature's crown!'

The trees swayed gently in a dance of age,
While the breeze wrote poems on life's yellowed page.
With laughter they echoed, from root to bough,
For humor's the trick that binds us somehow.

So gather around, let's hear the tales,
Of joy and mischief that never fails.
In every creak of wood and rustle of leaves,
The spirit of laughter is what nature weaves!

The Unseen Atlas of the Ground

Little critters plotting schemes,
Chasing ants, or so it seems.
A party lurks beneath the leaves,
With beds of moss, their favorite thieves.

A snail did make a map so grand,
But ended up in pudding sand.
His friends just laughed, they thought it sweet,
To find their buddy lost in treat.

The squirrels hoard their acorns tight,
In sunglasses, they munch with delight.
'Who needs the sun?' one shouted loud,
As shadows danced beneath the cloud.

And so beneath this leafy dome,
The groundlings claim their cozy home.
For every twig's a tale to spin,
Where laughter's found, let fun begin.

Beneath the Tranquil Overhead

A beetle rides a leaf like a boss,
Waving high, he's never at a loss.
'I'm the king of this green kingdom,' he declares,
While waving pompously at ants in pairs.

The worms all giggle, slipping in the mud,
Wagering on who'll win the next flood.
'Just wait,' says one, 'we'll party all day,
After the rain makes us squirm and sway!'

A grasshopper wearing a tiny hat,
Looks at his friends and says with a pat,
'Life is jumping, let's hop and skip,
We'll make this earth our grandest trip!'

So as they frolic, mud on their shoes,
Each moment bursts with laughter and views.
In the shade of leaves, fun takes its stand,
In their whimsical world, it's never bland.

Tales of Mossy Remembrance

Mossy beds with secrets old,
Whisper tales of bravery bold.
A worm once claimed he chewed a shoe,
Convinced that it was tasty too!

The mushrooms laughed, a clever crew,
While adding their own spin to the stew.
'He thinks he's brave, but look at him squirm,
His fashion sense is rather out of term!'

A rabbit hops in, ears all a-flap,
With stories far grander than a nap.
'Can you believe, I met a fox,
He wore a coat more stylish than crocs!'

And so through laughter, they reminisce,
The simplest joys are hard to miss.
With tales unique beneath the trees,
Mossy memories bring sweet unease.

The Earth's Quiet Reverie

The soil chuckles beneath my shoes,
As busy beetles share their news.
'Grass roots are in big gossip grips,
They claim the daisies steal all the tips!'

Shy mushrooms peek from their homes below,
Whispering secrets the ants might know.
'Come closer, come nearer!' they softly plead,
'We've got tales of worms who love speed!'

A frog croaks in between the fray,
'I wasn't invited to this play!'
The critters laugh as they gather 'round,
To spin wild tales from the dark, rich ground.

In this world of giggles, deep and wide,
Joy blooms softly, nowhere to hide.
With every root and wriggly friend,
The earth's sweet mirth shall never end.

The Cradle of Clay

In a patch of mud, I found a shoe,
In the dance of dirt, it stuck like glue.
Frogs wore it proud, as they jumped about,
Laughing at squirrels, who rolled their snout.

A worm pokes out with a cheeky grin,
'Why so serious, come join the spin!'
The ants are marching, a parade in line,
Stepping on crumbs, all feeling fine.

Mushrooms giggle in their polka dot caps,
As shadowy figures take silly naps.
A squirrel joins in with a little prance,
While beetles join feet in a bug ballet dance.

The wind starts to whistle a cheeky tune,
As pinecone maracas shake to the moon.
With every squish of the soft, wet ground,
Nature's whoopee cushions abound all around.

Scented Silences

In the shady nooks where fragrances play,
Lie dandelions dreaming the day away.
Bees in a buzz, they concoct their brew,
While daisies snicker at the weak and few.

A snail with sass claims the path is his,
Sliding along like he owns the biz.
'I'm the deep thinker of the green and the brown,'
He calls to a frog wearing mud for a crown.

The sweet smell of pine makes the bear feel bold,
While skunks gossip secrets, all stinky and old.
Whispers of flowers on a lazy breeze,
Telling tall tales with the greatest of ease.

But laughter erupts at the blushing blooms,
As bees misinform and gossip the rooms.
'There goes the skunk, oh such a surprise!'
They urge all the flowers to cover their eyes.

Echoes of Old Oaks

Beneath old oaks that have seen it all,
A squirrel is plotting his biggest fall.
He eyes a thick branch and takes a deep breath,
While chattering frantically as he flings himself.

'Look at him go!' says a wise old crow,
'When he lands, he'll surely put on quite a show.'
And just as expected, he wobbles and spins,
While the laughter of leaves breaks out from within.

Mice wear tiny capes, zooming round in haste,
While judging the skill of the squirrel's wild race.
A dash and a tumble, and then he takes flight,
Landing right next to the mushrooms so bright.

With echoes of laughter that drift to the sky,
The oaks just giggle, their branches swaying high.
In the heart of their roots, old stories unfurl,
Of acorns, mischief, and swords made of swirl.

Raindrop Reverie

A raindrop fell, with a curious plop,
Jumping on leaves, it didn't want to stop.
Puddles formed quickly, a waltz just begun,
As worms rushed in for a splash and a run.

The frogs lined up for a song and a muse,
Wobbling their voices in sloshing blue shoes.
They croaked and they ribbited, all in good cheer,
While tendrils of mist brought in whispers near.

The slugs set the stage for a slippery show,
Sliding between raindrops, all juicy and slow.
'The more we glide, the more we explore!'
Giggled the gang, as they searched for more.

While droplets danced freely on spider silk threads,
The bubblegum air filled the dreams in their heads.
Let's embrace the chaos of wet, wild delight,
For tomorrow brings sunshine and laughter in sight.

The Tread of Tiny Feet

In the damp of the woods, I hear them scurry,
Little feet skitter, without any worry.
A squirrel flips nuts with a flick of his tail,
While ants march on by, a well-practiced trail.

A rabbit hops by, with a twitch of its ear,
Dashing through ferns, filled with nothing but cheer.
They race through the leaves, such a comical sight,
Making me giggle, what a joyful delight!

A turtle moves slow, with a shell like a door,
While a ladybug giggles, "Why rush? There's much more!"
They dance in the dew, with a bounce and a twirl,
Nature's own party, a whimsical whirl.

Oh, the merry parade on this soft, leafy bed,
With acorns for hats and a pinecone for bread.
I sit and I watch, and I can't help but grin,
For life here is joyful, let the fun times begin!

Wonders in the Understory

Under the leaves where the sunlight is sparse,
The mushrooms grow tall, oh, what an odd farce!
With polka-dot hats, they seem ready to dance,
While spiders weave tales that put you in a trance.

A snail slides by, with its home on its back,
Trying to race, like it's on a fast track.
"Don't hurry," I chuckle, "you're doing just fine,
There's beauty in slime, and it's likely divine!"

The grasshoppers chirp, like a band out of tune,
While crickets provide a night song to the moon.
Beetles in tuxedos are strutting about,
With each little bug, there's no room for doubt.

In the shadows and tangles, such wonders await,
With laughter and joy, there's no need to be late.
I tiptoe through tales where the odd creatures play,
In this lush little realm, it's a fine holiday!

Whimsy of Worn Leaves

The leaves lie scattered, a quilt on the ground,
Each one a story, a treasure I've found.
Some are crispy, some crinkly, what a grand show,
Like nature's confetti, all gold, red, and brown.

I toss them in air, let the breezes decide,
Like a playful breeze wants a leaf to slide.
A fox thinks it sly, as he leaps through the bed,
Collecting his bounty, bright caps on his head!

The dandelions giggle, "Come play with the rest!"
While thistles just fume, feeling terribly stressed.
"Oh chill out!" I cry, "Let's make this a ball!
With twirls in the air, you'll not fuss at all!"

As shadows grow long, and giggles do fade,
I gather my treasures from this leafy parade.
Each whimsically worn leaf, a memory passed,
I'll tuck them away, but the fun's here to last!

Chronicles of the Cold Ground

In the chill of the morn, the frost paints its tale,
With sparkles of magic that sparkle and sail.
A raccoon, oh dear, with a mask like a thief,
Searches for truffles, then vanishes in grief.

The ground crunches softly under paw, hoof, and claw,
With critters in coats of the finest faux fur.
A hedgehog rolls by, all prickly and round,
And giggles erupt from the creatures around.

"Keep up with the gossip, we need the latest scoop!
What's that? Snails in tuxedos?" They form a small group.

With whispers and chuckles, tales of old woes,
How the frost bubble wraps all the small toes.

So here in this kingdom where frost gems abound,
Each creature's a storyteller, joyfully crowned.
I'll waddle back home with dreams freshly spun,
For the chronicles here are a chortling run!

Critters in the Darkness

In shadows deep where crickets sing,
A raccoon schemes a midnight fling.
With paws that swipe at crumbs galore,
    He dances near the kitchen door.

A squirrel peeks, his eyes so wide,
He giggles as the cat bolts inside.
The owl just hoots, with laughter free,
    As mice all join the jubilee.

Beneath the moon, where mischief brews,
A fox debates which snack to choose.
While hedgehogs huddle, trading quips,
    In secret spots that they eclipse.

So when the night invites a stroll,
Expect some antics, that's the goal.
Critters living life with flair,
    In the darkness, fun's laid bare.

Mossy Memories

Upon the rocks, the moss does bloom,
A soft green blanket, nature's room.
But underneath, a snail does plot,
His slow, sly scheme to steal the pot.

A toadstool tosses jokes around,
As mushrooms giggle on the ground.
They reminisce of rainy days,
When they all danced in puddled plays.

The lichen whispers tales of yore,
Of vagrant winds and muddy lore.
While ladybugs recount their trips,
In tiny giggles, sharing quips.

Memories of the sun's warm glow,
Where slugs and snails become the show.
What joy there is in this green mess,
Among the blooms of soft duress.

The Dance of Dappled Light

A sunbeam pokes through leaves above,
Where shadows play, the woods do love.
The light does waltz with every shade,
In a ballet that nature made.

A squirrel twirls, his tail a plume,
As grassy sways, the flowers bloom.
He bounces back with playful charms,
Avoids the dance with busy farms.

The bumblebees, all buzzing cheer,
Join in the fun, they've nothing to fear.
With pollen dust on tiny feet,
They groove about, their moves are sweet.

But watch the shadows! What a sight!
Ah, there's a bear who joins the fight.
He stumbles on, with quite the flair,
While mockingbirds jest without a care.

Hidden Paths of Pine

In winding trails, where whispers weave,
A squirrel hides a stash, believe!
Pine needles rustle, secrets shared,
With witty pines who've always cared.

The turtles trot in silly lines,
With shells that glimmer, stories shine.
"Who knew," says one, "we'd end up here?
What's next? A picnic, or a beer?"

Old roots chuckle, memories deep,
As shadows hug the woods asleep.
The wind brings laughter through the green,
In hidden paths, where fun is seen.

"Incredible sights!" the branches call,
"Where pine and critters link us all!"
So if you wander, take a peek,
In every nook, there's joy to seek.

The Life Beneath

Beneath the ground, the critters dwell,
With wriggly worms that twist and swell.
A party in the dark, they munch and crunch,
While ants in tuxedos prepare for lunch.

A beetle's dance, a ladybug's spin,
Mice in their jackets, let the fun begin!
They cheer for the rain, they hail the muck,
And laugh at the leaves that fall with a cluck.

Squirrels stop by to tell their tales,
Of pesky owls and wily snails.
With acorn hats, they toast to the sky,
While mushrooms giggle, oh so spry.

In this underworld of jolly glee,
Where no one cares, but all feel free.
Life's a laugh; it's more than a chore,
In the lively world that lies below the floor.

Canvas of Shadows

Painted leaves, a canvas so bright,
Where shadows dance in the fading light.
A spider's web, an artful display,
It catches the sun in a cheeky way.

Frogs in pajamas croak a tune,
Disco balls echo the light of the moon.
While toads tap dance on a branch,
Claiming the night as their very own chance.

Bees buzzing round like they earned a degree,
Polling the flowers, so lovely and free.
The fireflies twinkle, they're stars on a spree,
With their glow-in-the-dark parties by the old cedar tree.

Oh, what a show in this shadowy land,
With every critter lending a hand.
The canvas shifts as the stories unfold,
Where funny and silly are worth more than gold.

Underneath the Loam

Down in the dirt, where the giggles enhance,
Earthworms wiggle and take a chance.
They play hide and seek, but they're always found,
Poking their heads from the soft, rich ground.

Tiny turtles throw a shell-top spree,
While gophers read gossip under the tree.
"Mice plan a marathon, or so I hear,
And rabbits line up with a bit of cheer!"

Roly-poly bugs tumble and roll,
Creating a chaos that's hard to control.
While ladybugs nod with their spots all aglow,
Encouraging silliness from high to low.

In the loam, life's a whimsical game,
Where earthlings delight in fortune and fame.
And laughter echoes from roots up to skies,
In this funny world where no one complies.

Conversations with the Caterpillars

Caterpillars sit, with manners so fine,
Chit-chat about leaves and sunshine divine.
"Did you hear about Fred? He's getting quite fat!
He thinks he'll be a butterfly! Imagine that!"

They nibble and munch on a fresh, green meal,
Giggling together, with plenty to steal.
"Just wait 'til we fly, we'll show them our flair!
A parade in the breeze, oh, the sights we will share!"

With stripes and spots, they dream up their fate,
Swapping their secrets while trimming their weight.
"I'll be polka-dotted, you'll sparkle and shine,
Ditch these fuzzy coats; we'll look so divine!"

As twilight descends, they weave tales anew,
Of soaring above, in skies of bright blue.
In the grassy patch, their laughter takes wing,
Conversations of wonder, oh, the joy that they bring!

The Stillness of the Ground

Amidst the roots, I spy a snail,
With swagger slow, he leaves a trail.
A dance of ants, all in a line,
Marching to a rhythm, oh so fine.

A mushroom grins, all dressed in spots,
He's throwing shade at tired knots.
A beetle laughs, he rolls a leaf,
As if it's gold, beyond belief!

A rabbit hops, then trips a bit,
Cursing the grass, 'You little twit!'
While flowers nod with sunny glee,
They're gossiping about the bee.

So down below, the laughter grows,
In secret realms where no one knows.
The ground, a stage, where all can play,
In muddy boots, we end the day.

Bits of Bramble

Twisted vines weave tales so bright,
Of critters caught in a comedic fight.
A raccoon's mask, a bandit's flair,
Stealing berries, without a care.

A thistle pricked a passing fox,
Now he's frolicking like a paradox.
The brambles whisper, 'Don't be shy,'
While butterflies applaud, oh my!

They tangle legs in a wobbly race,
Bouncing off daisies, oh what a place!
A spider spins with a silken grin,
Writing poems on a leaf's thin skin.

In every thorn a giggle hides,
As nature's mischief laughs and glides.
Bits of bramble, stories share,
In this wild, whimsical affair.

Hints of Humus

A pile of leaves, a secret mound,
Where earthworms plot without a sound.
With wriggly tips, they curl and sway,
In the mud, they make their play.

A ladybug perched, oh so grand,
Supervising all with a tiny hand.
In the soil, the secrets dwell,
In hints of humus, tales they tell.

A tiny rabbit munches on greens,
While dreaming of pastures, fit for queens.
The compost crumbles, a cozy bed,
For dreams of carrots dance in head.

Here's magic brewed in earthy tones,
Where life breaks down from sticks and stones.
Hints of humus, laughter spread,
In tiny worlds beneath our tread.

Light Through Leaves

Sunshine dances, flickers bright,
Peeking through the leaves, what a sight!
Shadows play tag on the ground,
While giggles swish, no fear is found.

Squirrels chatter, executing leaps,
Gathering acorns, counting heaps.
A deer bounds softly, just for kicks,
As a chipmunk makes his silly tricks.

A fluttering moth joins the parade,
Whirling in sunlight, a joyful escapade.
Leaves rustle with a secret cheer,
As sunshine whispers, "Live, my dear!"

In the dance of light, no frown remains,
With every ray, joy never wanes.
Light filters down, a playful tease,
In nature's heart, where laughter frees.

A Symphony of Decay and Growth

In the shadows, a fungus sings,
Moldy molds with crafty things.
Toadstools dance, a merry crowd,
While worms plot mischief, feeling proud.

Squirrels chatter, oh what a show,
Chewing nuts, they steal the dough.
Ants parade in a line so neat,
While slugs slide by on slippery feet.

A leaf sneezes, falls with flair,
Landing right on a grumpy hare.
Mushrooms giggle, playing their part,
In nature's play, a comedic art.

Underneath this canopy bright,
Chaos reigns but feels so right.
Life and laughter, a playful swirl,
In this world of decay, we twirl.